FRANKLIN
the STILLBORN STATE
and the SEVIER/TIPTON POLITICAL FEUD

Dave Foster

ISBN 0-9644613-0-7
Published by Top Tenn Press, Inc.
(423) 429-1548 or (407) 422-0455
E-Mail: toptennpr@aol.com
Web site: http://members.ao1.com/toptennpr
Printed in the United States of America

2 3 4 5 6 7 8 9 0

Illustrations by Erick Foster

FOREWORD

In their drive toward statehood, the early Western North Carolina settlers took a detour down a dead-end road. They called it the State of Franklin. Today, we know the area as Upper East Tennessee.

We review the actions of the two main players of the saga that prompted a military confrontation in the 1780's. John Sevier favored Franklin while John Tipton remained loyal to North Carolina.

Dave Foster

The vast and foreboding Western frontier offered the early pioneers risks as well as rewards.

The Risks: Rugged wilderness, family separation, and warlike Indians.

The Rewards: Cheap farmland and the freedom to make a fresh start.

FRANKLIN
the STILLBORN STATE
and the SEVIER/TIPTON POLITICAL FEUD

Thirteen former British colonies, newly independent, called themselves the United States. They operated under a set of loosely drawn Articles of Confederation without the benefit of a constitution. Large numbers of war veterans, adventurers and land speculators flocked to the rich, unsettled river valleys of the Southwestern Appalachian frontier.

The Revolutionary War had ended, but many problems continued. Times were difficult in the 1780's. People lacked confidence in the inflated paper money that "wasn't worth a Continental."

Coonskins served as currency in the Southwestern back country. The pioneers paid taxes and settled their debts with animal pelts and farm products, but a person's land holdings measured his real wealth.

Speculators, led by William Blount, pushed the "Land Grab Act of 1783" through the North Carolina Assembly. That state wanted to pluck the value from its fruitful Western lands before turning it over to Congress. During a seven-month period of 1784 the land office sold almost four million acres at five dollars per hundred acres (in today's money equivalent). After many requests from the Continental Congress, North Carolina ceded its lands west of the mountain ridges during April 1784. This act opened four years of political intrigue and uncertainty for the area. See TIMELINE of FRANKLIN EVENTS on page 23 and MAPS on page 25.

The ceded territory stretched westward from the Appalachian

watershed to the Mississippi River and included all of present-day Tennessee. The act allowed Congress one year to confirm the proposal, as it called for certain financial and other concessions.

Pending acceptance by Congress, the ceded lands would remain under North Carolina's sovereignty, even though the Creek, Cherokee and Chickasaw Nations claimed most of the territory.

Strapped for hard cash, North Carolina asked Congress to credit it with the Indian War costs. It specified that, should a new state organize on the ceded land, the new entity absorb a portion of the public debt according to the value of the land. The act also stipulated that the total worth of the western lands, evaluated before the transfer, must count toward the Mother State's share of Revolutionary War debts.The western pioneers had good reasons to separate from the mother state.

> The western pioneers had good reasons to separate from the mother state.

North Carolina had promised to pay for land bought from the warlike Cherokees, but had not delivered. The Indians, aided and abetted by the British army, menaced the frontiersmen during the late Revolutionary War. Although these acts of terrorism continued, North Carolina offered little help to the frontiersmen, due to the state's poor financial condition.

The westerners had other complaints about courts and taxes. North Carolina refused to support an appellate court west of the mountains and unfairly taxed the western settlers.

Lands throughout the state carried the same tax assessment valuation. Landowners paid the same state tax per acre, whether on the productive farms on the eastern planes or on the rough undeveloped, tree-covered, western slopes. This formula unduly burdened the western pioneer settlers, prompting complaints that they received little in return for the taxes paid to the state. Had they not fought the recent war with England for a similar cause? In their minds the Mother State had deserted the overmountain men, the same who had gained the stunning victory at King's Mountain and thereby brought about a crucial turning point in the Revolutionary War.

With growing talk of a new state, many Western Carolina people eagerly welcomed the prospect of a more responsive government. Encouraged by North Carolina's ceding act, nine representatives from the western counties met with leaders from southwest Virginia on August 23, 1784, to discuss the new situation. The group accomplished little at this Jonesborough meeting.

Electing John Sevier moderator, they set an organizational meeting date for September 16, 1784. Each county's militia would choose delegates. This new expanded group did not meet until November. With several delegates objecting to separation, the meeting broke up in confusion. They met again in Jonesborough on December 14, 1784. William Cocke moved that they form a new and distinct state, independent of North Carolina. The motion carried, receiving 28 "yea" and 15 "no" votes. John Sevier presided at this meeting.

Born in Augusta County, Virginia, on September 23, 1745, John Sevier moved to present-day upper East Tennessee in 1771 or 1772. Before coming to the frontier, he had bought land and developed the town of New Market, Virginia. Serving in positions of leadership in the frontier militia, he engaged in many Indian-warfare missions. He also led the overmountain troops to victory against the British in the 1780 battle of King's Mountain.

Before Congress could act on the proposed secession, a newly elected North Carolina Assembly met in October and repealed the act passed earlier in the year. This new legislature renewed the pledge to help with the settler's Cherokee problem and established a District Appellate Court to serve Greene, Sullivan and Washington counties. The westerners could now press their legal appeals without making a long and difficult trip over the mountains.

In the conciliatory move, Governor Alexander Martin named several individual leaders of the new-state movement to high office. He tapped David Campbell as the new Superior Court District Judge.

Before news of these actions arrived from east of the mountains, delegates from the three western counties had already held their December meeting and decided to form a separate state. The delegates adopted a temporary constitution, but allowed time for the citizens to study the proposal. They intended to adopt a permanent document for the new government after a period of public discussion. A third of the delegates wished to stay with the Mother State. John Tipton and his brother Joseph sided with the minority in the 28 to 15 vote count.

John Tipton, born in Baltimore County, Maryland on August 15, 1730, moved to the Virginia Frontier when he was a young man of seventeen. Engaging himself in local military and public affairs, he earned the rank of colonel in the militia and served as a recruiting and supply officer during the Revolutionary War. In civil affairs, he represented Shenandoah County in the Virginia House of Delegates from 1776 to 1780, and was a party to the Woodstock Declaration of Rights. He served as Justice of Peace and Sheriff before moving to the southwest frontier in 1783. Sevier and Tipton both lived in Shenandoah County at the same time. It is possible they met during the 1760's and 1770's before emigrating from Virginia to the frontier.

As indicated by the vote, John Tipton and a few other settlers hesitated to pull away from North Carolina's protection. Some pioneers believed that the mother state could better secure their land titles. The separation question prompted wide differences of opinion, as many farmers had settled on Cherokee land along the area's southwest borders.

The prime movers who favored cessation included Arthur and David Campbell, John Sevier, and Samuel Houston. Within days of the North Carolina Assembly meeting, John Sevier received three critically important items of news from east of the mountains. First, North Carolina had rescinded its land cession act, and second, the Assembly renewed its promise to speed up payment for the Indian land. The third piece of news involved Sevier personally: The governor had appointed him militia commander of the three-county district.

Upon receiving this information, Sevier decided that these corrective acts by the mother state would satisfy the settlers.

He urged his friends to back away from the new-state movement. However, William Cocke persuaded Sevier to go ahead with the separate government movement. At the first organizational meeting on March 1, 1785, Sevier's friends in the legislature elected him governor of the would-be state.

Was the name Frankland, or Franklin? Historic accounts are murky; settlers who lived in the area were often called Franks. John Sevier's ancestors came from France, which apparently accounted for the Frankland spelling. Sevier appealed to Benjamin Franklin's vanity when he requested help in birthing the state. He did this by referring to the State of Franklin in a letter. Benjamin Franklin responded to Sevier, stating that he had heard the proposed state's name was Frankland, not Franklin. At any rate, the idolized old sage of Philadelphia suggested that Sevier direct his appeal for help to North Carolina. He further suggested that Sevier not encroach on Indian territory, as Congress would not rush to Franklin's aid in case war came.

The new Franklin legislature's first act embraced a set of basic administrative laws. It soon added four new counties, including Wayne, Spencer, Sevier, and Caswell (later renamed Jefferson), all located in present-day upper east Tennessee. At this session it officially adopted Franklin as the state's name.

The Franklin legislature appointed David Campbell to head its Superior Court, the same role and function he would assume as Chief Judge of Washington District, North Carolina. The new state representatives asked William Cocke to plead their cause before Continental Congress. Additionally, the Franklin Legislature appointed John Sevier head of a commission to conduct talks with the Cherokee Nation.

Signing an agreement known as the Dumplin Creek Treaty on June 10, 1785, this Sevier Commission completed its work within three months. The pact with the Indians extended Franklin's southwest border. Now, instead of ending at the French Broad River, the boundary ran along the land ridge that divided the Little and Tennessee Rivers. The on-rush of settlers seemed to ignore the poorly defined line, which crossed present-day Blount County near Maryville.

Another serious problem of the Sevier treaty opened new difficulties between the Franklin settlers and Indians. Claiming they lacked proper representation, several older Cherokee chiefs insisted they had not agreed to the Dumplin Creek pact.

A few months later, during the fall of 1785, another treaty would present the frontier Franks with an issue of life or death importance. This involved an accord negotiated by the federal authorities at Hopewell, South Carolina. An agency of the Continental Congress, the commission signed an extensive treaty with the Cherokee and other frontier Indian nations. Two men from North Carolina, Joseph Martin and William Blount, represented their state in drawing up this new federal treaty. It dealt harshly with Franklin, the would-be state.

The commission negotiators obviously wanted to punish the Franks, for the Hopewell Treaty drew new boundaries that totally ignored the Dumplin Creek accord. They returned control of the recently Sevier-negotiated lands back to the Cherokees. Vast areas, including the territory around the newly situated Franklin capital city of Greeneville, reverted to Indian control.

The new treaty, nonetheless, protected the settlers along the Cumberland River in present-day Middle Tennessee. Clearly, the Federal negotiators intended this act to be an insult to the Franks. Dealing an even more striking blow to John Sevier's personal ambition, the Hopewell Treaty recognized the Creek Nation's sovereignty over the Muscle Shoals territory at the southern bend of the Tennessee River. John Sevier, in concert with others, had schemed to gain control of this prize fertile land for some time.

The treaty subjected some five thousand Franklin pioneers to jeopardy, especially those settlers living beyond the French Broad River. Within six months the entire territory would revert to the Indians, allowing the frontiersmen little time to move from the land. Afterward, the fate of the so-called intruders would rest solely with the Cherokees.

Franklin citizens, many of who had lived on the disputed land for years, ignored the federal treaty. The Cherokee Indians did not. Now, they could terrorize the pioneer settlers with impunity.

> Governor Martin called the legislative acts
> of Franklin a revolt.

When North Carolina Governor Martin learned of the meetings of the separatists and their motion toward self-government, he labeled the acts a revolt. Near the end of his term, he called a special session of the Assembly for April 25, 1785. When a quorum failed to attend, the matter had to await the regular fall meeting and a newly elected governor. Meanwhile, Gov. Martin issued a proclamation to the citizens of the Washington three-county district. He suggested that members of the fall Assembly could legally resolve the Franklin statehood problem, "Otherwise, blood will flow."

When Col. John Tipton of Washington County read the governor's proclamation he promptly signed a statement of loyalty to North Carolina and promised to, "continue to discountenance the lawless proceedings."

John Sevier responded differently; On May 15, 1785, he issued his own proclamation. He demanded that all Franklin citizens obey laws of the new state. These competing decrees spread confusion throughout the western district.

Five days after Sevier's edict, the Continental Congress took up Franklin's request for statehood. William Cocke, in pressing the case before Congress, requested that the new state include parts of present-day Tennessee, Kentucky, southwest Virginia plus the Muscle Shoals section of Alabama. Governor Patrick Henry pushed an act through the Virginia legislature in the fall of 1785 that declared the movement "high treason."

Congressional acceptance of the proposed state of Franklin required approval by nine member states. Since the state had not yet ratified the pending federal constitution, North Carolina did not vote on the matter, and Cocke could muster only seven votes. Congress referred the question to North Carolina.

This turn of events failed to shake the Franks. Meeting in August, they located the state capital at Greeneville and unleashed an extensive public debate about a proposed new permanent constitution. This quarrel over the document opened a broad schism, a split from which Franklin would not recover.

Samuel Houston, uncle to the Sam Houston of Texas fame, and others, including William Graham, proposed a strong democratic and religious constitution. It came loaded with many novel ideas for the time.

> Franklin's new constitution would exclude lawyers from legislative service.

Every man could vote regardless of his financial situation; Previously, a voter must meet certain requirements as to net worth or land ownership. All newly proposed general laws would become statutes only after six months of public scrutiny and debate. The governor would gain office by popular vote instead of appointment by the legislature. The new constitution called for a single house assembly without provision for a chief executive's veto and excluded lawyers from legislative service.

John Sevier came out against the proposed new constitution, possibly because John Tipton helped author the document. Houston promoted the document with a broad distribution of pamphlets that raised spirited passions on both sides. This pitted the Sevier group against many people who favored the initiative. Tipton's support intensified the political feud between himself and Sevier. Eventually the legislature failed to adopt the new constitution, leaving the temporary one in effect.

Meanwhile, a friend of John Sevier became governor of North Carolina. Richard Caswell and Sevier were business associates as well as friends. The two men, in partnership with four others, attempted to gain control of the fertile lands of northern Alabama. Late in 1784 they sponsored a new settlement in the Muscle Shoals area, but problems with the Indians doomed the project.

Once in office, Caswell offered amnesty to Sevier and other Franklin leaders. But first, they must end the rebellion and return their allegiance to North Carolina.

Local opposition against Franklin had remained reasonably subdued until the summer of 1786. The strongest support came from the lower frontier counties, but the Frank candidate of Washington County won a North Carolina Assembly seat, defeating John Tipton. This election, along with the failure of the popular constitution as proposed, provoked many ordinary citizens to action. Tipton's friends, including Houston, David Campbell, and James White, returned their loyalty to North Carolina. Franklin could offer nothing to this coalition with John Sevier calling the legislative shots.

Public discord in the region remained, but in another area of concern the settlers came together. The continuing acts of terror by the Cherokees alarmed and united the settlers. Such acts called for a militia muster, so officers met in Jonesborough to draw up plans. Sevier argued that the muster should come under Franklin's laws, but as commander of the Washington County, North Carolina Militia, Col. Tipton disagreed. He insisted the mother-state laws apply. The dispute escalated until the malice between the political enemies erupted into violence. Sevier

Sevier and Tipton Conflict Comes to Blows

struck the first blow with his cane and Tipton responded with his fists. Friends pulled the two combatants apart, but not before Tipton had gotten the upper hand, according to spectators.

In the fall of 1786, John Tipton regained his Washington County Senate seat. This Assembly, in a conciliatory mood toward the Franklin promoters, offered a full pardon to anyone who returned his loyalty. On the other hand, they declared to be vacant all the North Carolina governmental posts filled by individuals who were still in rebellion. The Assembly confirmed anew the military and civil appointments of 1784, but excluded those individuals who had served as Franklin officials. North Carolina also took an unusual action for any government. It agreed to return any land taxes collected within the past two years to people who lived in the disenfranchised western areas.

The popular Evan Shelby accepted an appointment as Militia Commander of the Washington District with the rank of brigadier general. He replaced John Sevier, who had held the office for two years while at the same time serving as Franklin's governor. Shelby and Sevier were neighbors and friends. Earlier, Evan Shelby had supported Franklin and put himself in rebellion, but now his acceptance of the North Carolina militia command ended his ties with Franklin. This military appointment prompted Shelby to shift back to the mother state and lead other citizens to reverse their patronage.

The brilliant political ploy by Governor Caswell failed to pacify everyone. Still angered by North Carolina's rejection of the new state, a group of hot heads hanged an effigy of John Tipton. Nonetheless, popular support for Franklin continued to erode.

General Shelby, hopeful of defusing and resolving the problem through compromise, called a meeting with Sevier and other Franks for March 20, 1787. These talks produced a novel idea. Each settler could decide for himself whether to pay taxes to Franklin or North Carolina. Shelby's efforts brought an immediate calm to the civil unrest, but the lull failed to last.

In the Spring of 1787, Franklin and North Carolina both held court in Hawkins, Sullivan, and Washington Counties. This promoted a keen competition between the two systems. John Tipton

**Pro-Franklin Hot Heads Hang Tipton in Effigy after he convinced
N.C. Legislature not to recognize Franklin.**

held the office of clerk of the court for Washington County, North Carolina at Buffalo. Meanwhile at Jonesborough, ten miles away, John Sevier's brother held the same office under Franklin.

Both factions attempted to exercise control over the local government. Many items concerned all citizens; these included the recording of wills, deeds and marriages. Civil and criminal cases required attention. Often a sheriff's work steered him across area boundaries. Perhaps a court might require legal papers on deposit with the other court. Jurisdictional conflicts between the two opposing sides erupted frequently.

On one such occasion, Tipton led a raid on Franklin's Jonesborough courthouse. Ordering the judges into the street, he took possession of certain court records. John Sevier retaliated. He used Franklin militia force to remove court records from the Buffalo, North Carolina courthouse.

The retaliation continued. In a show of force, the sheriff of Washington County, Franklin, threw Sheriff Jonathan Pugh, of Washington County, North Carolina, into jail.

Franklin's legislature met in the fall of 1787 and elected Evan Shelby governor. Although urged by his friend Sevier to accept, Shelby refused the office. Given the Mother State's conciliatory mood and Franklin's internal dissension, many supporters of the would-be new state changed their minds.

General Shelby resigned his commission as head of North Carolina Militia and recommended his friend Sevier as his replacement. Instead, Joseph Martin received the appointment. With its influential people deserting, the Franklin ship began to sink.

Political contention and strife continued to trouble the people of Greene, Spencer, and Washington counties. Citing an unpaid tax judgment against John Sevier in early 1788, a North Carolina judge ordered the impoundment of his stock and slaves. Sheriff Jonathan Pugh seized the property and delivered it to Tipton's farm for safe keeping.

This act, taken with Sevier away from home, sent him into a fit of rage. He assembled the militia, most of who lived in Franklin's three lower counties. They marched in late February 1788 ready to do battle.

In freezing weather, 135 militiamen trooped to the crisp beat of fife and drum behind John Sevier, Governor of the State of Franklin. He halted the force within view of the farm home of Colonel John Tipton, of the North Carolina Militia. A cold wind whipped through the Franklin ranks as the commander signaled an officer to ride forward. Sevier pulled a white handkerchief from his pocket and secured it to a long rifle. He handed the gun and a letter to the officer and instructed him to deliver the ultimatum to Tipton's door.

"You are to surrender within thirty minutes and submit to the laws of the State of Franklin." It was signed, John Sevier, Captain General.

While awaiting the response, Sevier's men began to set up camp in a low area some two hundred yards beyond the house. Scouts patrolled all the roads leading to and from the Tipton farm compound. A sergeant posted two guards on the old buffalo trail near an outcropping of limestone. The stage coach traveled this road between Jonesborough and Elizabethton and forded Sinking Creek near Tipton's. Sevier issued strict orders; no one was to pass without challenge.

A chilled sentry spoke to his companion near an outcropping of limestone, "I've served with him since King's Mountain and I ain't never seen Colonel Sevier so riled up. Them eyes were a'spitting fire when old Chucky Jack ordered the scouts out on patrol."

Soldiers of the main body dismounted and tied their horses to tree branches. The frontiersmen beat cold hands against their bodies and stomped frigid feet on the frozen ground, anything to protect themselves from the wintry blast. They gathered wood and built campfires.

Protecting themselves from the freezing weather became more important than the mission at hand. Their coonskin caps and double layers of homespun cloth under long deerskin hunting shirts failed to keep the men warm. A light snow blended with the howling wind to flicker the campfires. Nightfall came early as the gray sky faded into a dark blur of fog and snow.

Sevier received no reply other than a simple verbal statement from Tipton: "I ask no favors and if Sevier will surrender he will have the benefit of North Carolina law." Within a few moments a group of reinforcements arrived from the east. They drew fire from Sevier forces.

The deadly accurate musket fire spilled three of the arriving militiamen to the ground when their horses fell dead. A bullet struck one of two women as they walked from the house to the spring house. Screaming, the women dashed to the safety of the main house. Tipton and his added defenders did not return Sevier's random rifle fire.

Sevier enjoyed complete control of the military situation. With his cannon stationed near the site, he could blast the house apart with ease. After darkness fell, both sides settled in for a tense, and frigid, winter night.

Colonel Tipton, having learned earlier of Sevier's approach, had sent an express rider to solicit help from Colonel Maxwell, who commanded the Sullivan County Militia. Although Sevier's scouts patrolled the roads, Tipton managed to slip another messenger out to rally help from his local North Carolina militiamen. In the early morning hours, twelve of Tipton's friends sneaked into the house undetected.

Apparently, the sentries had vacated their post to warm themselves at the campfires. Later, Colonel Robert Love led eighteen more defenders into the farmhouse.

The stand-off continued into the dark winter night. Some thrity-five North Carolina militiamen sat poised to defend the compound under attack, but help was on the way.

Before dawn of the siege's second night, a patrol of Sevier's scouts, including two of his sons, galloped between the camp and Tipton's house. Riding in an easterly direction, they peppered the house with rifle fire, but caused little damage.

At that moment, a company of one hundred Militiamen commanded by Colonel Maxwell approached from Sullivan County. They arrived on the opposite side of Tipton's house from the bedded-down troops. The shots convinced Maxwell the battle had already begun, so he ordered his troops to dismount and attack the Sevier camp from the west.

Upon hearing the commotion and gunfire, Tipton led his men in a charge from the opposite direction. This pincer grip action, taking place in the darkness and a raging snow storm, surprised Sevier and his troops.

Startled by this attack from opposite directions, the Franklin troops fought briefly but soon scattered into the nearby woodlands. Tipton and his men pursued. They captured twenty or thirty soldiers and seized a quantity of camping equipment, including the artillery piece.

Sevier's returning scouts believed they were returning to their own camp, but rode into the arms of their captors. Tipton flew into a rage when his men brought Sevier's sons before him. He threatened to hold court, convict, and hang them on the spot, but Colonel Love interceded.

Sevier marshaled a few of his fleeing militia and retreated toward Jonesborough. Fearing for his personal safety, he sent Tipton a message. His verbal, white-flag message stated "If you spare my life, I will submit to the laws of North Carolina." In answer to Sevier's query, Tipton replied, "I will not take forceful advantage of the present situation."

Earlier, with his cannon aimed a Tipton's house, Sevier had held the upper hand. Now, the situation reversed. Whenever either of these longtime adversaries held the advantage over the other, he refused to exploit the situation. Militia troops on both sides hesitated to shoot at or kill his frontier neighbor. However, four people lost their lives in the battle. Tipton's losses included Sheriff Pugh, who succumbed to wounds a few days after the battle. Within a few days Tipton paroled all captives, including Sevier's sons.

After this debacle at Tipton's place, Sevier found himself in an untenable position. Important local people shifted their allegiance back to North Carolina. Franklin faded.

Sevier, in spite of his battlefield pledge to recant Franklin, refused to give in and continued to rally his followers. Meanwhile, the Indians continued their killing, pillaging, and burning in the areas ceded them by the Federal Hopewell Treaty.

The Franklin legislature, claiming self-defense against the Indians, authorized John Sevier to call up the militia. Considering the past mischief caused by two sets of county officials, two sets of courts and two sets of opposing militia commands, the

Carolina supporters viewed this act as a grim prelude to civil war.

General Martin summoned Colonel Tipton and the militia commanders of Sullivan and Hawkins Counties to a military parley. The growing unrest demanded swift action. After the meeting, General Martin requested that Governor Caswell augment his militia force with 1,000 additional troops immediately and suggested that Caswell appeal to Patrick Henry, the governor of Virginia, for rapid military assistance.

Governor Caswell refused Martin's request for more troops. Instead, he wrote an open letter to the Franks and sent a personal note to John Sevier. Preaching restraint, the governor suggested the opposing parties could resolve the Franklin quarrel at the next Assembly meeting without spilling a drop of blood. This wise political measure calmed the discord.

Sevier decided to take Benjamin Franklin's suggestion; he would attempt to persuade the mother state authorities to accept the issue of statehood. He stood for election to the North Carolina Senate from Greene County and won. The people of Washington County elected John Tipton.

Other serious problems demanded Sevier's immediate attention. For nearly two years he had corresponded with Georgia officials, soliciting help to develop the lands he coveted. He failed to attend the Assembly because this long-standing plan faltered.

Georgia had declared war on the Creek Indians who controlled the choice lands Sevier wanted to develop. He promised to furnish the Georgia governor with up to 1,500 Franklin troops to further the scheme. The troops would protect the settlers moving to the area. The project languished because Georgia also suffered from economic strife. Sevier requested funds needed to cover campaign expenses, but the money never came.

A new development in Georgia would alter his well-nurtured plans, for that state ratified the federal constitution and joined the Union. This changed everything. The western territory, including the targeted lands, would now fall under United States federal jurisdiction, and President George Washington wanted peace with the Indian nations.

This event dashed Sevier's grand designs for developing the

Muscle Shoals area. Georgia would not go to war with the Creeks, so they had no need of the Franklin militiamen. Given this development, Sevier had no further need for Franklin.

Another event struck a blow at Sevier's faltering popularity during the spring of 1788. It involved Indian attacks. The John Kirk family lived a few miles south of Knoxville. One day when Kirk and his oldest son were away, Indians attacked their home, killed and scalped eleven family members. At almost the same time, when Colonel James Brown, his two sons and five other men drifted down the Tennessee River, Indian bushwhackers attacked and killed them all.

These wanton acts of slaughter raised fear among the whites that a general Indian uprising was at hand. Sevier swung into action. He called the Franklin militia and prepared to take revenge against the Indian villages to the South.

General Joseph Martin, Commander of North Carolina Militia, attempted to calm the fears of both settlers and Indians. The general was married to a daughter of Nancy Ward, a powerful Indian princess. Given his involvement with the Hopewell Treaty and close association with Indians, neither white man nor Indian had confidence in General Martin.

Martin heard of the militia muster. When he traveled to the Indian town of Chote on the Little Tennessee River, the General stopped by Sevier's staging camp and issued orders for Sevier to abandon his military plans, but to no avail. Nothing could dissuade Sevier from his plan to sack the Indian villages. The braves who butchered the Kirk family lived at Chilhowee, so that village became the main target.

Sevier sent a message to Old Tassel, the main Cherokee chief west of the mountains and a long-time friend to the white man. He asked the chief to come in, to arrange for safe travel, and to go with the military procession to Chilhowee. Once there, they would pow-wow with other chiefs from the surrounding areas.

Sevier sent Major James Hubbard ahead of the main party accompanied by Old Tassel. John Kirk, Junior, also joined the lead group. Under a truce flag arranged by Old Tassel, the entourage peacefully traveled through Indian territory. They crossed the Hiwassee River and entered the village of Chilhowee without difficulty.

Hubbard gathered the assembled chiefs in the tribal counsel building for the meeting. Once safely inside, he posted guards around the structure and handed Kirk a tomahawk, saying, "Now you can take your revenge."

With this invitation, the enraged Kirk plunged his vindictive tomahawk into Old Tassel's head. The other chieftains sensed that their captors had used the white flag to trick and double-cross both Old Tassel and themselves. Offering no resistance, they lowered their heads and yielded their lives with pride and dignity as Kirk murdered them one by one.

Kirk Takes Revenge on Old Tassel and Other Chiefs

Arriving soon after the massacre, Sevier chastised Hubbard and Kirk on the spot. However, lacking military status, he could not place court martial charges against the two men.

Upon receiving news of the slaughter, Tipton suggested that Sevier had condoned the massacre. Though Sevier had gained his prestige among the pioneers as an Indian fighter, he claimed innocence in the matter. Later, in a letter of exoneration, Kirk accepted total blame for the action. However, the incident devalued Sevier's reputation with President Washington, who had wanted to keep peace with the frontier Indians. The president called Sevier an Indian murderer.

> Governor Johnson ordered John Sevier arrested and charged with treason.

General Martin reported the details of Sevier's actions to Governor Samuel Johnson. North Carolina's new governor would not tolerate this failure to follow orders nor the wanton acts of murdering friendly chiefs. He ordered Sevier arrested and charged with treason. Judge Spencer of Washington County, after another judge had refused to act on the request, validated the arrest warrant and passed it to Colonel John Tipton for action.

Sevier's arrest stirred up public support for the popular Indian fighter. Responding to the likelihood of angry mob reaction, Tipton decided to move the prisoner to a secure district for trial. When guards delivered Sevier beyond the mountains to Morganton, Colonel Charles McDowell came to Sevier's aid. A friend since the King's Mountain campaign, he posted bail and secured Sevier's release. The treason case never came to trial because of the general amnesty passed by North Carolina's Assembly.

Three months after Kirk slaughtered Old Tassel, John Tipton took his seat in the July 1788 North Carolina Senate. The Assembly debated whether to endorse the Federal Constitution. They pondered the yet unresolved war debt and the proposed Constitution's lack of safeguards for individual liberty. To this question they voted no, but sentiment in the Assembly toward Franklin began to mellow. They granted a general amnesty that included all former belligerents. However, with John Tipton pushing it, the legislature excluded John Sevier from the holding of any governmental office. Nevertheless, the general pardon included the former governor of Franklin.

During this period of low self esteem, Sevier fell into a gloomy mood. He began to drink excessively. With Franklin's future in doubt, Sevier desperately fanned its dying embers to ignite a

Tipton Arrests Sevier for Treason

dangerous venture. In September 1788, some six months after his term as governor had expired and just weeks before his arrest, Sevier entered into a correspondence with Diego de Gardoqui, a Spanish diplomat. He did this, knowing that he was under a charge of treason.

At the time, Spain controlled the vast region that stretched from Florida and the Gulf of Mexico to include present-day Louisiana, Mississippi and Alabama. Sevier sent an official letter to the Spanish diplomat, suggesting that the citizens of Franklin would welcome an alliance with the King of Spain. He listed Franklin's three main terms for such a framework. They included: free commercial navigation on the Mississippi River, expansion of Franklin's boundaries to include the Muscle Shoals area, and a hard currency loan to be repaid by tariffs collected at Spanish ports. Sevier suggested that Franklin's foremost citizens would pledge allegiance to Spain, but stipulated that they must manage their own internal domestic affairs.

Attempting to save Franklin in one stroke, Sevier still aimed to salvage his long-held designs on the fertile land of northern Alabama. Ultimately, in a letter dated April 1789, Governor Miro of Spanish New Orleans responded to Sevier's initiative. Since peace existed between his country and the United States, the Spanish governor refused to buy the proposed annexation scheme.

Franklin died a slow death. In October of 1788, after John Sevier had returned from Morganton, its remnant held a final meeting near Seymour in Sevier County. Even though he swore allegiance to North Carolina in February 1789, Sevier continued his service to the would-be state. He acted as the defacto Indian commissioner and military leader.

In January of 1789, Sevier won a stunning victory over a pack of marauding Indians at Flint Creek and restored his popularity with the settlers. This win, coupled with the Assembly's attempts to tell the Greene County residents, who could—or could not—represent them, raised Sevier's fortunes in the eyes of his neighbors. They elected him to the next North Carolina Senate, in spite of the law that excluded him from the holding of government office. John Tipton would represent Washington

County at the same Fayetteville assembly.

Sevier refused to claim his seat immediately, but waited for his friends to pave the way. This ploy worked. Within days, the assembly repealed the act that excluded Sevier. Now the two adversaries, Tipton and Sevier, sat together in the North Carolina Senate as they had on the board of Washington College Academy.

North Carolina ratified the federal constitution and, for a second time, ceded its western lands to the United States. The ceded land became The Territory of the United States South of the Ohio River. President Washington appointed William Blount governor of the new territory.

> # John Tipton would help write Tennessee's constitution and John Sevier would become the first governor.

Both John Sevier and John Tipton, following their political feud over the would-be state of Franklin, would play important roles in birthing a new state. After seven years of territory status, Tipton would help write Tennessee's constitution, as he had done years earlier for Virginia. Sevier would become the sixteenth state's first governor. Their political associations on opposite sides of the fence continued after Tennessee joined the Union. Tipton and his sons strongly supported fellow Tennessean Andrew Jackson's bid for the presidency, but Sevier remained their political enemy.

The idea of self government by the people was still a new idea in the America of the 1780's. The Franklin feud between Sevier and Tipton ushered a new type of rivalry on America's western political landscape. For more than two centuries now, political parties have vied for the spin-offs and spoils when their friends are elected to high office. Truly, Sevier and Tipton were authentic pioneers of the southwestern frontier, but as midwives at Franklin's stillborn birth, they also served as political pioneers.

TIME LINE of FRANKLIN EVENTS

1780   James Robertson leads settlers to Cumberland River Valley and Nashville area.

Revolutionary War King's Mountain victory led by Isaac Shelby and John Sevier.

1781   Virginia cedes Continental Congress its vast territory northwest of Ohio River.

1782   John Sevier appointed Clerk of Washington County, North Carolina.

Cornwallis Surrenders to George Washington at Yorktown, Virginia.

1783   John Tipton moves from Shenandoah Valley to Watauga frontier.

Greene County founded by dividing Washington County.

1784   North Carolina conditionally cedes its western territory to Continental Congress.

Representatives gather for first Franklin organization meeting.

North Carolina revokes the act that gives up its western territory.

1785   Franklin legislature organizes and appoints John Sevier governor.

Sevier - Tipton argument about a militia call up ends in a fist fight.

Continental Congress refuses to admit Franklin to United States.

Hopewell (Federal) Treaty gives southern Franklin land to Cherokees.

1786   North Carolina Governor Caswell offers pardon to all Franklin rebels who recant.

Hawkins County, N.C. established.

William Cocke unsuccessfully pleads Franklin's case before N.C. Assembly.

1787   Governor Caswell appoints Evan Shelby Washington District Militia Commander.

U.S. Constitution Convention ends, Gen. Shelby meets with Sevier in effort to avoid war.

N.C. Court orders Sheriff Pugh to seize Sevier's property.

1788 Sevier with Franklin militia attacks Tipton's farm.

Gov. Samuel Johnson orders Sevier's arrest for treason following the Kirk affair

Franklin Legislature holds final meeting in Sevier County.

United States becomes a nation.

1789 George Washington inaugurated first President of the United States of America.

N.C. ratifies Federal Constitution and cedes its western lands for the second time.

1790 United States Territory South of the Ohio River formed, Wm. Blount appointed Governor.

1791 Governor Blount signs U. S. Holston Treaty with Cherokee Nation.

1792

1793 Sevier and Tipton elected to Southwest Territory's first legislature.

1794

1795 Territory legislature asks John Tipton to help write a constitution for a new state.

1796 Tennessee becomes 16th State, Tipton elected Senator and Sevier appointed Governor.

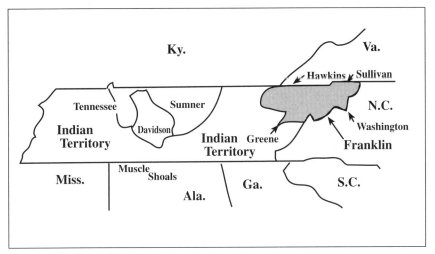

**Western North Carolina Counties
and Franklin During the Mid 1780's**

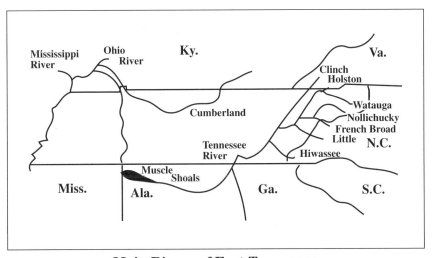

Main Rivers of East Tennessee

AUTHOR'S NOTE:

Many historians have studied the Franklin experience, but few have examined its political fallout. My essay is different in that I attempt to describe the political thoughts and moves of two main characters, John Sevier and John Tipton, based on the events. My research, plowing through yellowed pages of history books and other data, convinces me that historians see events through idiosyncratic eyes. I've tried to look at Franklin and its political setting through the mind of John Tipton, the lesser known of the two main players. My work draws on some likely, or plausible, sentiments that may have crossed the minds of these high-spirited leaders during the saga. Making a few suppositions, I've looked for motives to explain the acts of historical men.

If you wish to examine the question of Franklin further, you might check the following sources:

* *Tennessee — A History*, Philip Hammer, American Historical Society
* *McClung Collection Tipton Folders*, Entitled Allen, Parham and Genealogy located at the Lawson-McGhee Library, Knoxville, Tennessee.
* *The Overmountain Men*, Pat Alderman
* *Winning the West*, Theodore Roosevelt
* *The Lost State of Franklin*, Samuel Cole Williams
* *Annals of Tennessee*, Dr. J. G. M. Ramsey
* *Tennessee — A Short History*, 2nd Edition, Robert E. Corlew
* *East Tennessee's Lore of Yesteryear*, Emma Deane Smith Trent
* *Tennessee — A Bicentennial History*, Wilma Dykeman
* *John Sevier, Pioneer of the Old South*, Carl Driver
* *History of Washington County*, 1988, James T. Dykes, Editor